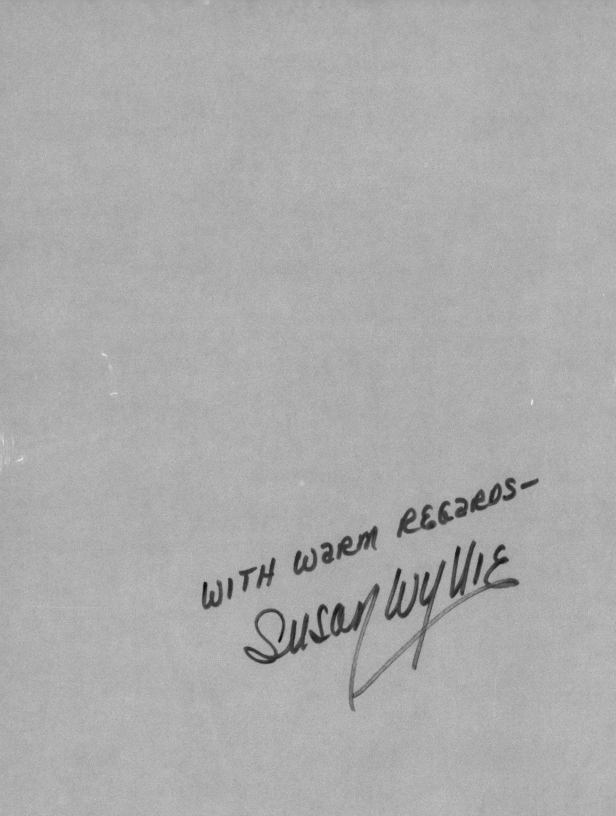

WITH WARM REGARDS—

Susan Wyllie

WITH WARM REGARDS -

[signature]

The Inner Game of Beauty

Volume 1: Winning

The Inner Game of Beauty

Volume 1: Winning

SUSAN WYLLIE

EDITED BY
Patricia Cannon
Lauree Kuhlmann
Kathryn Smoot Caldwell
John K.M. Olsen

ILLUSTRATED BY
Mary Newbold

COVER DESIGN BY
Smith + Clarkson Design

ISBN: 0-934126-85-2

First Printing
September 1985

Lithographed in the United States of America
TYPOGRAPHY BY EXECUTYPE
Salt Lake City, Utah

Dedication

To the other voice that was once my opponent.

The Score Is Love/Love

Life served us our role,
>and even when we hit back
The return often slammed
>beyond our reach.

Who was this opponent?
>How could it know my moves
To always be where I was?
>To connect so easily with my lob?

I couldn't fool it,
>I couldn't match its strength,
I couldn't find its weakness.
>I couldn't wait out its patience.

"Is there any way to win?"
>I asked myself;
And then my coach's voice:
>"Know thine enemy!"

I waved to my opponent
>to come to the net.
I shook its hand and
>felt to congratulate it.

Our eyes met
>and with horror I saw
That I stood face to face
>with me—that face was mine!

I was opposing myself
>all this time.
The endless volleying
>might never end.

Now I knew how strong,
        how clever I was.
I had never given in
        or refused to play.

But if I win
        it loses, and if it wins,
I lose—the game is over.
        Either way, it's a loss.

What is the answer?
        How do we win?
There is no way
        unless

We join our energies
        and play on the same side.
Our opponent would be life
        which plays hard, for real.

Together, we can cover
        the court's breadth
And return every serve
        which life affords.

The game of beauty is won
        when the beauty inside
Joins the beauty outside
        as a partner of the Self's creation.

                    —Susan Wyllie
                    August 1985

Preface

"THIS can change your life. . ."
Words you and I hear spoken about everything from childbirth to meditation. But sometimes my life *is* changed. It happens just often enough to keep me on the lookout for *the* sensational experience.

To know Susan Wyllie is such an experience. Watch reactions as she enters a room; feel the instinctive group recognition of a woman who carries about her an air of subdued excitement. Then note the light diminish as she exits—that's the most telling of the signs of her charisma.

Many who envy this charisma discount it by calling it a trait—some people are born with it, some not, like green eyes or left-handedness. Susie, as she is often called, knows better. She's created her magnetism. It's the product of an inner renaissance followed by a quest for personal awareness that continues even now. From it Susie has distilled her secret: she knows what makes a woman beautiful.

She doesn't want to keep this knowledge a secret; it's Susie's nature to want to share her good news. It became the basis of her understanding of the struggle for a meaningful inner awareness, individually conceptualized, understood and felt through a process of discovering a personal connection to color. This process was conceptualized by Susie into a seminar. Women who have participated in these learning experiences asked the same questions over and over: "How did Susie do it?" "How did she arrive at such an understanding?" And so this book was written in answer to those voices.

The following is the story of Susie's struggle to master what was a mystery. I acknowledge her courage and determination, her tenacity in pursuing her dream. My admiration led me to one of those life-changing experiences—the kind that, once it happens, nothing is ever the same.

I was co-facilitating workshops in interpersonal communications. I felt my life was in order—I certainly didn't need another seminar. But Susie was a friend; I decided to take the seminar she was teaching on a lark . . . and ended up re-working my entire self-concept from the inside out!

The first thing I discovered was how selfish I had been in my use of color, wearing colors that protected me rather than colors that created harmony for those who viewed me. This was important information for me because of my very visible position as a people-helper. The colors I had been choosing for myself were based on my self-image. I had been told that my eyes were a ghastly color, my skin tone ruddy and so I chose colors that would de-emphasize my eyes, drain away the ruddiness of my face. What I was doing was hiding; hiding behind an old belief system that women aren't supposed to be as assertive, influential and powerful as my position required. I learned from Susie I was creating distraction because I was unwilling to acknowledge myself as a source of such power. I was using powerful colors to avoid responsibility for my own capabilities.

Susie awakened me to my inner game-playing. Afterward I was able to choose a more responsible course. I began to use the science of color and design principles as powerful resources, to reveal my Self instead of hiding. And I discovered I liked that Self.

I also liked the response to that Self from friends and those with whom I work. I continue to be Susie's friend, among the throng of women and men who have benefitted from her work.

Susie's story is one you will enjoy; it will uplift you as you share her journey . . . as it has me. Thanks, Susie, for sharing the struggle.

—Lauree Kuhlmann

Introduction

MAKE me beautiful! What a strange idea. Does it mean paint over me as you would a piece of furniture? Many a fine piece of furniture has been ruined that way, when a thick coat of paint covers the natural grain of the wood.

Beauty is a natural part of the world. It is a natural part of each of us. We are many colors— colors which harmonize to make up our own unique beauty. Color isn't something to be coated on; it is something to bring out—as *part* of our beauty.

What is it that each of us wants to bring out, to show the world the part of us that matters? We know what it is when we are children; somehow, many of us lose this understanding of ourselves as we grow up.

Let me tell you of an experience that happened to me when I was a small child. Something similar might have happened to you. I had a beautiful baby pink dress, one of the prettiest dresses I ever had—as long as it was on the hanger. I hated to wear it. I felt that people were looking at me when I wore it, and perhaps it was because I didn't want that much attention, or perhaps I thought they were only looking at the dress and not me—but I hated it. I kept looking down at that dress; I couldn't for a moment forget that I had it on, so that I was even unable to talk to people. I couldn't think about them or what they were saying. I could only think about that pink dress that my body had on.

That dress didn't have anything to do with the me that was inside. The color, the style, had nothing to do with me. Wearing it is the first memory I have of not being beautiful, of realizing something was wrong about my appearance. Now I know it was the dress, not me, that wasn't "right."

Now I would never allow that to happen. Now I am connected to what I wear, its color, its style, the total effect. It's all me, and so I am able to forget my clothes, my make-up—my total outward appearance. Beyond that final nod to the mirror as I leave home (a self-approving nod), I don't think about how I look. That leaves me free to get to know other people, to enjoy the world beyond myself. What a wonderful feeling!

I wasn't always like this; I wasn't free. From that incident when I was a child wearing that awful pink dress, to this point, today, has been a difficult trek. I thought I was ugly and I blamed the people who loved me most for the way I felt. Then I learned the enemy was really me. I was the one telling me I was ugly, unworthy. I was the one who sent me to "experts" to help me be better, to "paint on" the beauty I was missing. So my challenge was to get myself to know me—and to love me.

It isn't an easy task when you're used to listening only to critical, negative comments about yourself, to begin listening to the positive—and then to listen primarily to what *you* have to say to yourself. It's hard to take so much responsibility when you're used to handing over your self-esteem to others' care and labeling. It isn't easy, but it's worth the trip. And it is the only way you will ever free yourself to become as beautiful as only *you* can be.

I know because I have taken that trek; I have had your same questions and your same fears—and as ugly as *you* feel some days, I know I felt uglier. No one has ever been fatter, pastier, more freckled and with crookeder teeth than I—at least that's what I thought. If you think those kinds of negative, awful— completely erroneous—thoughts about yourself, then let me share my story with you. Let me tell you how one woman helped herself to the beauty that was there the entire time.

Chapter One

MIKE Douglas turned to Clint Eastwood, "Is it true that you're as much an introvert in real life as on the screen?"

"Well, uh, Mike, you know that everything you read in the tabloids isn't true. . . ."

The television blurred. Six-year-old Erica switched the channel to Sesame Street and turned up the volume. John, Jr., 8, chased Kirsta, 4, on to the sofa to retrieve his pop gun, tipping over a full box of Cheerios that had been teetering precariously on the end table.

Unmoved, I closed my eyes in dull despair. It was too rainy for the children to play outside . . . and I usually enjoyed playing with them. But I was simply too depressed today—I wasn't even sure why. If I could only sleep.

Then came the knocking. Was that little William pounding his plastic hammer on the hardwood floor again?

Louder knocking. Dazed, then startled, I leaned over to look out the window. Oh, no! Some fancy woman at the door! I couldn't possibly answer it.

There I sat in the rag I called a bathrobe, with no make-up, my hair in curlers, the children running around in their pajamas and my living room strewn with toys and cereal. How could I let anyone see me in such a mess at 11 o'clock in the morning?

More knocking. Before I could catch her, my four-year-old had swung open the front door. There stood the PTA President from the children's school. She saw me before I could hide. I gulped hard, went to the door and invited her in.

Passing by the mirror, I caught a look at me—a real hag . . . like the "before" in a "before and after."

Blushing, I swept several Cheerios off a chair so she could sit down.

"Don't worry, dear, I won't stay but a minute," she said.

Fumbling with my curlers, I forced a smile. "Sorry about the mess; it's been one of those days." (What I didn't tell her was that *every* day was becoming one of those days.)

"I just stopped by to see if you will be the chairman of our school Christmas party."

I gulped again, "Well, yes, sure," hoping to speed her departure. I could read her mind: "Susie is so sloppy. So fat. And these children look like orphans . . . the house is a *disaster!*"

She stayed only a few minutes, but it was an eternity to me.

I fought back the anger and tears at being caught in such disarray—until she left.

Then it all came out—on the children. "If you aren't dressed in five minutes, you'll go without lunch," I screamed. "Clean up that cereal before I count to three, or you'll spend the rest of the day in your room." Four frightened little people scurried

"We but half express ourselves, and are ashamed of that divine idea which each of us represents."
—*Ralph Waldo Emerson*

12

into all parts of the house.

It wasn't until a few hours later that I calmed down sufficiently to see the absurdity of punishing the children for my own embarrassment.

Then I relived in my mind the visit from the PTA President, and much to my dismay, realized how ungracious and unfriendly I had been to her. My debilitating self-consciousness had stood between us like a brick wall. That painful event was typical of many other occasions in a life marred by low self-esteem.

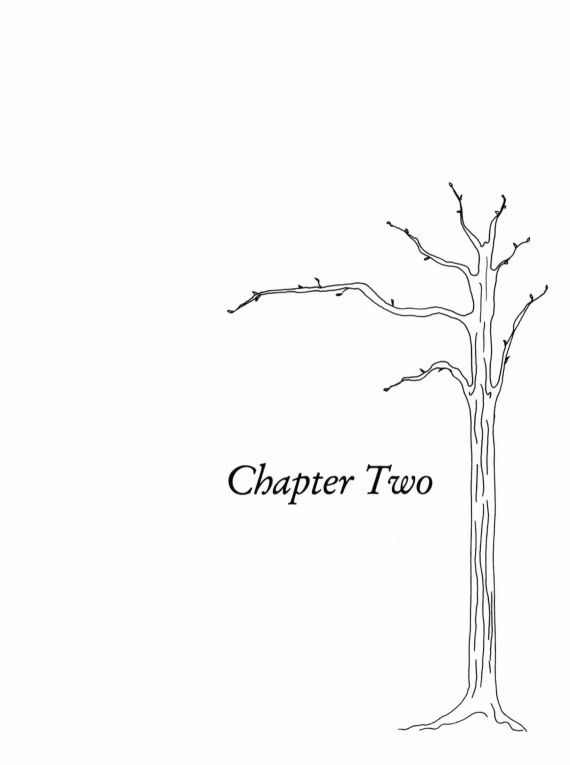

Chapter Two

GROWING up I would hear daily comments such as: "How can you be so stupid?" "You're going to be fat just like your grandmother!" "You'll have a 'potato nose' if you don't stop rubbing it." "You're such a baby! Why don't you grow up?"

Even as a child, my self-focus was negative. When I looked in the mirror I saw a fat girl with a big nose, unmanageably curly hair, crooked teeth, hairy arms, and pasty white skin—just another zero in a doomed world.

Many of the critical comments came from my father. Mother stood silently by unwilling to inter-fere.

My home was not unlike that of Archie and Edith Bunker; perhaps the difference was that it was not a TV sit-com with an audience laughing in the background. It was real, and there was no laughter.

I remember in grade school having continual nightmares about snakes in my bed. I'd run teary-eyed to my parents. My father's typically adult response: "How idiotic! Don't be ridiculous! There aren't any snakes in your bed. Get back to sleep!" So I would feel my way back into the darkness of my room alone, look under the bed, then carefully under the covers, then sleep on top of the blankets to protect myself from phantom snakes, and cry myself to sleep.

NIGHTMARE

I turned the light out
and rushed to my bed,
Pulled the covers
Nearly over my head,
And hoped the "Boogie Man"
Wouldn't get me!

I wouldn't dare open my eyes
Because the shadows in the room,
At the window, in the doorway,
All hovered over me.
"Hurry, sleep, come save me.
Take me away to safety!"

My eyes closed, but my mind raced.
Then slowly I drifted into space. . .
Aware, but not touching my bed.
So peaceful for a moment. . .
I don't even know
How many precious minutes.

Then the nightmare began!
Before long those shadows
Had taken on form.
They crawled in bed with me
And were squirming around.
"Help! Help! Mother! Daddy!"

I raced to their room
Afraid to even put one foot
In front of the other. . .
I might step on one.
They were all over my bed,
The floor, everywhere!!!

"Daddy, there are snakes in my bed!!"
My heart was pounding so loud.
Did I hear him right?
"That's ridiculous!
Get back in your bed!"
"Daddy, you didn't hear me."

—S.W., Aug. '84

My father's comments hurt, but he was my father, so I believed him—the world and I were simply ridiculous and stupid.

I felt I was an embattled soldier on enemy territory all the time I was growing up.

My sister Monica was four years old when I came along. By then she had received a curative dose of Daddy's harsh discipline. When she was a toddler he didn't want her going near the stairs in the new house my parents were renting. So whenever she approached the stairway, Daddy spanked her.

Monica learned to obey our father. She's been obedient ever since.

Luckily for me, Mother decided there would be no more harsh physical punishment and protected me from the fate of my sister.

To this day I can hear my father: "You're nothing but a spoiled brat because you never got the discipline you deserved!"

I'm not sure that even now I can fully appreciate the personal sacrifices Mother made for my sister and me.

In the eyes of my parents, Monica could do no wrong. She was so good, so sweet, so perfect. She had the ability to bend; I didn't. So I created a lot of commotion at home, sassing and standing up to my father's irrational hatred for life and "all the idiots out there" who were part of it.

But not Monica. She demurred to his ranting and, to my eleven-year-old mind, she seemed perfect with her pretty little nose, straight teeth, long, slender hands and fingernails and a beautiful, modest figure. I felt dumpy by comparison. At age eleven I was humiliated at being so fully developed that I had to get my bras from the "old lady" stores.

Monica's obedience caused me to appear the brat by comparison. We fought incessantly until she married and moved away. I grieved when she left, sobbing at her wedding. It was only then that I realized how much I needed her friendship.

I was lonely. I believed I was unattractive, worthless and probably even to blame for all the unhappiness in my family. Sometimes I wondered, "If I were prettier, would everything be okay?" Cinderella had a hard life that became a dream-come-true because she was pretty and she was good (and she had a Fairy Godmother). Her step-sisters were ugly, and they were bad. Maybe I was unhappy because I was so ugly. If I could be pretty, would I live "happily ever after?"

As a teenager in the fifties, as with most teenagers of any decade, it was important for me to fit in with the crowd. Straight teeth and straight pageboy hair was essential. I had crooked teeth and curly hair. Jantzen sweaters, tweed skirts and Joyce shoes were the rage. We couldn't afford them. Even if we could have, my father said it was stupid to want what everyone else had.

At age thirteen I begged Daddy to let me have braces. My two eye teeth stuck out like fangs. I would never smile in public because of them.

I nagged endlessly, making everyone's life miserable. But I begged to no avail.

"Hell, no, you don't want store-bought teeth like all those idiots out there," was Daddy's only response, referring to my friends who had worn braces.

I didn't give up. I finally wore my father down, and he said I could have braces. I was sixteen.

Even after such a delay I was overjoyed, until the day he took me to the orthodontist.

"She can have braces, but only if you take them off before her teeth are straight," Daddy told him. "I don't want her going around looking like every other mouth you damned dentists send out on the streets!"

I couldn't believe my ears! I was so embarrassed.

How could he do this just to teach me the "realities of life," as he put it? We had no money. He borrowed money for the braces and then made certain it was done his way.

He made sure I did many other things "his" way. School sororities and Friday night dances were the life and breath of all my friends in high school. I was forbidden to participate. They were obviously not for me if everyone else was involved.

The unwritten rule: If it brought happiness, I couldn't have it. My father's reasoning was that any kind of happiness is temporary, so why bother with it?

"I don't care if you're happy," he said. "I'm not raising you to love me, but to learn to do without. Then when you leave home, you'll always be able to live with nothing. And if you think you'll ever have anything, you're fooling yourself. Don't count on it!"

Mother tried to compensate for the lack of money and my critical father. When I was in high school, she agonized at the sewing machine to make me a dress for the Junior Prom.

I wanted this dress so much; I had begged Mother to make it, and I chose the pattern. It was a tiered formal made with yards and yards of stiff white horse-hair net. She worked hard on it—without much help from me.

I was in a world of my own, unconsciously trying to put together a better self-image. I felt unfinished and raw around the edges, just like that net formal. The special dress would make everything different. I, like Cinderella, would look the way I had always dreamed.

But as the dress slowly took shape, reality took over: I would be noticed all right—but not because I was Cinderella. How could my mother have done this—made my dream real—a nightmare? How could I be so ungrateful? (*Where* was my Fairy Godmother?)

What could everyone see . . . my unfinished seams? They'd know I didn't belong.

"Well, forget that thought, Susan!" I told myself. "Your date is special; concentrate on him. *Pretend* and it will be all right."

The dress grew worse once it was finished. By the night of the dance I saw it as too obviously homemade. When I put it on, it felt like a huge, white tutu. I died a thousand deaths the night I wore it. But I pretended I was thrilled, and I lied to my mother. I told her I loved it, which was half true. I loved *her*. She believed me. There was a hideous part of me that tried to hate her for loving me that much. Now I would be embarrassed, and it was all her fault. I just couldn't handle being noticed.

My date, of course, said I was radiant that night! So I pretended to be radiant. Then we walked in to the dance. Dave, Lynda's date, said, "Wow!" Lynda just beamed! I was embarrassed. Everyone said I looked absolutely, unbelievably, exquisitely beautiful. But I knew what they were thinking. In my mind they were saying gushy words—you know the ones that are said with that certain *emphasis*—when what they mean is, "Poor girl, if she could only see herself." And, "She tried so hard."

My date was kind all evening while I was thinking, "Why do I even try to be pretty?" and "Look at Diane, she's a natural beauty. She was born with it. Just look at Nancy. She is so vibrant. Why am I so plain?"

I knew I didn't look plain that night—just plain absurd.

"Be patient with everyone, but above all with yourself. I mean, do not be disturbed because of your imperfections, and always rise up bravely from a fall."
—Sir Francis de Sales

Despite my feelings about homemade clothes, mine were. Or they were bought on sale, or hand-me-downs. I tried to tell myself it didn't matter. But it did. I knew everyone at school was looking down on me because of what I wore.

But as lonely as I was at school, it was nothing like the isolation I felt at home.

So I concentrated all my energies on getting straight A's. Getting good grades and the approval of my teachers was the key to my survival emotionally, because it was the only positive thing in my life at the time.

But even my academic success became a factor in my being outcast from the group.

"Here comes Susan with her homework all done, as usual."

"Hey, computer brain!"

How ironic that my friends made fun of me for being so smart, while my father made jokes about stupidity. The one way I could find to please him was to keep up the grades.

What I would have given to be held in my father's arms and told, "You don't have to be afraid, because we love you and understand."

I couldn't help but notice how carefree my friends seemed, even around their parents, who were so open with their affection. What could bring this freedom and affection into my life?

How could I change my parents? *How* could I change myself? *What* should I do? *Where* should I

"When you remove the masks, take away the defenses, doubts, guilts, and inhibitions, you find a beautiful person waiting to experience life—emotionally, spiritually and creatively."
—Powell Buxton

24

start?

I was forever plagued with one question: Would I ever amount to anything? Despite predictions to the contrary, a calm, reassuring voice within me kept saying, "Yes."

It took nearly forty years of my life for me to trust that voice completely.

Chapter Three

DESPITE my poor self-image, I developed leadership qualities in my drive to be responsible. As a high school junior, I was nominated to be the representative for Long Beach Polytechnic High School at California Girls State, a large gathering of high school junior girls from across the state, selected by community leaders to experience the democratic process in a one-week marathon of mock conventions, campaigning and state elections.

I was surprised at the honor, and *shocked* when elected Governor. I had found a place in the world. But the real test came when there was trouble, the next year at Girls State.

The first two days of the conference the adult counselors had been telling me that they'd never worked with such a difficult group. Many there were unreasonably ambitious in their campaign to be the next governor. The politics had taken on a negative theme that cast a pall over the whole group.

I felt responsible because I was the outgoing governor. And true to my upbringing, I believed it was all my fault.

One day, while all two hundred girls were at lunch in the cafeteria, I walked alone into the huge dormitory where all of us had our bunks. I found mine and anguished over how to handle the situation.

I wasn't sure where the thoughts telling me what to do came from. All I know is I left the dorm, walked slowly but confidently into the cafeteria, past all the girls, past the head table where I was to sit with the advisors, and stepped up to the microphone.

Gripping the podium until my knuckles turned white, I closed my eyes for a moment, and heard myself begin, "Your attention, please . . . I have something to say." Then I proceeded to deliver a message to the crowd that, to this day, I don't really know the contents of.

Afterward, when I read comments pressed into my hand, it was obvious the words I had spoken had come from a source I had never known before.

I knew something profound had happened when I saw tears in the girls' eyes as I sat down. That week Girls State became a roaring success. At the end of the week, at the autographing party, my book filled up rapidly. Before leaving for home, I read a couple of the inscriptions:

> "Susie, I shall think of you as I enter Church each Sunday morning, for you're one girl who walks with God. I sometimes hear His voice in your smile." J.B.

> "Amid fear and anxiety and that dreadful feeling of the lonely who yearn to belong, you spoke. You spoke of your own fear, and those of us who were afraid were comforted in knowing that we were not alone. 'Give of yourselves,' you said. And we listened. You spoke of our selfishness and thoughtlessness, but with such tenderness and wisdom and love we could but cry and vow to never be hurtful again. As my life goes by, if my smile can contain a little of your sparkle, if my eyes can glow with only part of the warmth of love that shines in yours, if my life can enrich tens in the

"A smile is the key that opens a closed up heart."
—Unknown

30

way yours has enriched hundreds, I will surely find happiness." C.O.

Me, a source of strength and inspiration? Not possible—I felt so totally inadequate. I was stunned by the response of my hundreds of new friends to a speech that I couldn't even take the credit for.

I went home only half-believing what had happened, certain that it had all been some kind of mistake, especially when I received the expected dose of cynicism: "Well, Susan, now that all that Girls State attention is over with, maybe you can get on with real life."

I couldn't and wouldn't share my special new feelings with my parents—this time they weren't going to spoil it for me.

The rest of that summer I was consumed with preparations to enter Stanford University, excited and frightened at the same time by many new thoughts. My parents had wanted me to live at home and attend one of the smaller colleges, but when I was accepted at Stanford, I knew in my heart there was no alternative for me.

I had never even imagined I could go away to such a prestigious school, but my counselors convinced me to apply. After submitting my admittance application, I was afraid I wouldn't be accepted, at the same time panicky that I would. If I wasn't accepted, I would know it showed that I was a nothing. If I was accepted, I knew they'd find out I was nothing when I got there.

Though my counselors wanted me to apply for a scholarship, as they were sure I would qualify, my father was too proud to fill out the application forms. He took out a loan to do it "his way." He said no one was going to pay for his child's education. That confused me for years. I called it false pride and thought he was being unreasonable. But I was determined to prove my worth by earning money.

While babysitting, I vacuumed, folded laundry, cleaned the refrigerator—I really went all out. As a result, I was the most popular babysitter around. It was a chance for me to fantasize about how it would be when I was a homemaker and mother. It was a great escape, and I lost myself in it. I pretended I was the perfect wife and mother. My pretense game was getting better, too.

In my spare time I tried putting together a wardrobe for the coming school year. Shopping with Mother was usually not very fun. No matter what we brought home, Mother's fears were supported as we were met by my father's predictable response. "Why in the hell did you get *THAT*? It's useless."

I think it's a miracle we ever went shopping at all. Thank goodness I had hand-me-downs to wear and a mother who kept going against all odds.

Girls State had given me a taste of self-awareness and excitement for life I had not previously known. And going away to a big university would surely mean more of the same. But I was frightened. The conflicting voices were at it again in my head, and the real serious game of inner war was wearing me down.

Was I the revered former Governor of Girls State

"Even a turtle doesn't get ahead unless he sticks his neck out."
          —Unknown

or the serious, fat girl with pasty white skin, hairy arms, curly hair, a potato nose and not-quite straight enough teeth?

I was afraid to find out.

Chapter Four

IN the beginning Stanford was not a happy experience. I was challenged by my peers and professors to think for myself, but I was too insecure to enjoy the privilege.

Every time I had stated my thoughts at home they were labeled "stupid," so I found independent thinking almost impossible. I had stifled my instincts for so many years I was unable to think freely, convinced that my thoughts were inadequate and inaccurate.

The only thing I was aware of that first quarter was how miserable and frightened I was. But I couldn't tell my parents. I knew I'd have to find happiness on my own. The question was: How does a blob go about finding happiness?

In high school I hadn't done much dating, but in college I had plenty of dates because the ratio of men to women at Stanford was three to one. I discounted my success, believing it was due to the numbers, so it was no particular boost to my self-esteem.

One night during the second quarter, I went to a party with a classmate. He began drinking heavily and became so obnoxious that I asked him to take me home. He refused.

My only alternative was to ride home with another couple. I was humiliated, sitting in the back seat alone.

When I arrived on campus, I ran crying into my dorm. Another girl was there signing in. She asked me what was wrong. I didn't tell her, but her warm invitation to come cry on her shoulder sounded pretty good right then.

She listened, and I was impressed by her genuine warmth. The following week she lined me up with a young man and we double-dated to San Francisco for dinner and a show. The three of them sang happily all the way. How could they be *singing*? I wondered. What makes them so happy? Where was the phoniness, drunkenness, and pseudo-intellectualism of my other classmates?

Was it possible to sing and laugh without drinking yourself silly in a smoke-filled room?

Instantly I felt comfortable. "This is wonderful. Everything's okay." I was actually smiling.

The world wasn't doomed after all, and neither was I. Such feelings are just as real as negative ones—a new realization for me. It felt good. But the consequences were frightening: My new awareness would make me even more unacceptable to my father, who thought the only way he could have fun was to soften reality with a few drinks.

During that second quarter a friend introduced me to John K. M. Olsen, a senior at Stanford Law School.

After a few weeks, we had our first date. He was the proverbial tall-dark-and-handsome, and much more. I couldn't explain my profound new feelings, but when I arrived at the dorm that night, I announced to my friends, "I'm going to marry him!"

I was as shocked by my own comment as they were. John was ten years older than I. He was accomplished, well-travelled, educated, stable and handsome. I felt I was nobody by comparison.

What's more, he was already involved in a relationship with a very beautiful girl. But she lived out of town, and he saw her only on school vacations.

I was the one he took on study breaks. We'd go for ice cream or a bite to eat, then back to the books. We became good friends. And with all our other friends, I felt loved and accepted for the first time in my life.

John's other girlfriend was everything I wasn't— tall, slender, beautiful, sophisticated, with blonde hair slicked back in a bun, showing off her lovely features, including a perfect nose.

When I first met her she was on her way to Europe, dressed like a magazine model. John would certainly want to marry someone like her.

But my feelings of inferiority were buoyed up by the safe, predictable friendships which seemed to evolve naturally among my new friends. I was riding on the crest of my discovery that life *could* be happy.

My new way of life seemed like a fairy tale, but I still feared the old negatives that loomed like storm threats on the edges of my life.

Then came the inevitable reckoning with my father, and the storm broke.

Home for summer vacation, I tiptoed my way through an explanation of my new attitudes, my friends—how they had taught me to look at life in a positive way.

"How could you be so stupid as to be conned into that damned bunch of nonsense? There you go again, letting your emotions run your life."

His cold remarks brought me down with a crash.

"Go ahead, get it out of your system. In a few months you'll see it for the idiocy that it is. On second thought, maybe I won't send you back to Stanford. With your narrow attitude you'll never learn anything."

I was crushed by the power he still had over me. Trying to please him while staying loyal to my new friends and my new ideas left me in constant turmoil.

Loud arguments were again a way of life at home during the long summer break. My mother, who would have peace at any price, sat by crying, probably believing it was all her fault.

John and I dated off and on that summer, with his beautiful girlfriend tucked neatly away in Europe. He was consistently calm and kind—a perfect contrast to life at home . . . my only respite. I enjoyed but felt unworthy of the blossoming friendship.

When my father allowed me to return to Stanford in the fall, it was like being released from jail. Such relief and joy! I plunged back into my chosen course of study, Speech Pathology and Audiology, determined to bring up my grades which had suffered somewhat while I had learned to play the last quarter.

My social life took a permanent turn for the

"The greatest battle of life is fought out within the silent chambers of the soul. A victory on the inside of a [wo]man's heart is worth a hundred conquests on the battlefield of life. To be master of yourself is the best guarantee that you will be master of the situation. Know thyself. The crown of character is self-control."
—Unknown

better. There was always something wonderful
happening, always with fun, stimulating new friends.
I was accepted and loved, and I felt free to love in
return. There were picnics, hiking, parties and
rehearsals for plays and musicals.

Then came the surprise. After an eight-month
friendship, John proposed to me! I said, "Yes."

My mother was the first of my parents to learn
of the engagement. She didn't know what to
say. She seemed so uncomfortable during that brief
phone conversation. Perhaps she feared I was
jumping into marriage too quickly. Or was she
worried about my father's reaction?

As I was talking to my mother, my father was
returning from a trip to Chicago. He came by to see
me unannounced and totally unexpected. After
having the front desk ring my dorm room, he walked
around the lobby. Stopping briefly to scrutinize a
bouquet of red roses, he noticed a card at the foot of
the vase announcing the engagement of Susan Wyllie
to John K. M. Olsen. He had left for his trip to
Chicago with the mistaken notion that surely nothing
too earthshaking would happen while he was gone.
What must have gone through his mind I can only
imagine.

What could I say? What would be brilliantly
reassuring as I walked into the lobby and saw my dad
reading that card? I was so happy a few minutes ago,
but seeing him—the look on his face—kept me from
saying, "Daddy, I'm happy. This wonderful man
actually wants to marry *me*, your daughter." I did
manage to bring on a smile as I met him eagerly.

The next day my father took John to lunch and

made himself very clear. "You are in for hard times. I think you're making a big mistake. Your backgrounds are so different—and the differences are irreconcilable. It will never work."

Nevertheless, we were married six weeks later, during the Christmas season, in the quaint Stanford Memorial Chapel. I was told my father got drunk that night.

Chapter Five

I N the depths of my insecurity, I was amazed that a man of John K.'s background, experience and stability would choose to marry me. I was still immature and vulnerable.

But he passed the true test of patience and endurance during the ensuing years as I frantically searched for my identity.

I still saw myself as a worthless, fat, boring, stupid woman with pasty white skin, hairy arms, a potato nose, too-curly hair and not-quite straight teeth. John didn't help matters by his teasing about my short, broad feet with stubby toes. I saw it as another flaw that hadn't come to my attention before now. Still, I knew that somewhere inside, there was a glamorous, exciting person clawing to find her way out.

John couldn't understand the effects of my negative childhood. Our courtship had been short, and I doubt he had seen the full extent of my internal conflict.

I remember an earlier attempt to share some private feelings of inadequacy one night on a date. "Nobody really likes me. They just put up with me because I tag along with you." Such feelings were foreign to John.

"What are you talking about? Don't be ridiculous," he said.

I misinterpreted the comment as criticism and began to keep my feelings hidden. During our courtship, I did such a good job of covering up that he couldn't believe I was anything but strong.

We couldn't have been more opposite. John was pragmatic and analytical; I was emotional and eclectic. I had never witnessed first-hand a healthy marriage in action; consequently, I didn't know how to respond constructively to conflict.

My low self-esteem caused me to constantly strive for John's approval. I was crushed by every tiny negative comment that I imagined came my way. I'd cry buckets of tears and feel inadequate for days. What was wrong with me? Why did I turn my feelings over to another person? I would interpret his comments as criticism and crumble under his tone of voice. He would try to encourage me by telling me it was silly to feel this way, a remark I felt was another put-down.

I believed he was telling me that my feelings were invalid—wrong to have. Then I'd panic over his disapproval and be overcome by my fear of being left alone. That's when I'd put a smile on my face, a fresh apron over my dress and go about the business of a busy homemaker, as though nothing had happened. As long as I did the "acceptable thing," perhaps I wouldn't lose him.

In one of our more painfilled encounters, John gently suggested that I seek professional help because he couldn't help me. So I went to a psychiatrist. At first, I took John's suggestion as the harshest criticism of all—but, for people who've gone for a long time unable to safely disclose their heartfelt feelings and insecurities, therapy can be helpful, as it was for me. It took a long time to acknowledge that I *did* need help, and I *did* need to learn about myself.

Meantime, I wondered in agony how I could ever get out of the self-defeating trap I felt I was in.

I reflected on my mother's long-suffering loyalty and constancy through her own emotional pain. Though her problems were different than mine, I was inspired by her quiet strength. Somehow she had stuck with my father through all their misery. She was a model of endurance for me.

"You cannot teach a man anything. You can only help him to discover it within himself."
—*Galileo*

After several years of painful encounters, John and I realized our marriage would require changes on both our parts. It would be hard. Happy endings were only in story books. John had lived a controlled life and didn't understand other peoples' feelings. I had lived a life of compressed rebellion and emotionality. We soon learned the distance between feelings is the loneliest road to travel.

DISTANCE

Our childhoods were
Worlds apart
But we bridged this
With the commonality of insecurity.

How close we drew
With a promise of loyalty,
Strangely, to support each
Within his own lost world.

But that meant
Permanent distance—
Not physical, not spiritual—
Only a gaping emotional abyss.

Where is the lifeline?
What is the road to travel
That will join two alone
Who went separate ways?

How distant do you get
Before it's too far,
Too late, to grasp
The cry of longing

To be understood,
To be needed,
To be wanted.
The cry seems to echo.

I long for
The touch of closeness
That distance denies.
How far away is love?

—S.W., Aug. '84

How could we bridge this distance? Could John learn to become more flexible and expressive?

Simultaneously, could I learn to become less explosive and emotional—more tolerant?

No one would dispute that I was difficult to live with; despite John's frustration with my insecurities, he retained his belief in me. I was still a valuable person to him. He encouraged me to grow and delighted in any accomplishment I made.

I *had* grown since leaving my parents years before, but somehow my low opinion of myself remained the nemesis of my life.

Perhaps that's why I took such comfort in our children.

Eleven months after we married, I gave birth to our first son, Johnny. He was a delightfully easy baby. We were very relaxed with him and took him everywhere with us. Nearly two years later, Erica was born, then came Kirsta. I seldom resented being tied down with three babies. That was my time and season for motherhood, and I enjoyed it, as much as it was possible for me to enjoy anything at that time.

And being a busy mother allowed me to forget about my sagging sense of self-worth—for awhile.

I'd always wanted a big family, and we kept having children. (By the time we were through, we had Johnny in college, Erica in high school, Kirsta in junior high, William and Trevor in elementary school, Katrina in kindergarten and Amanda in nursery school!)

The children were my best friends. They boosted my self-esteem because they saw me for myself and loved me anyway.

Johnny, our oldest child, knew when I was down and always came through with some words of reassurance and cheer. He'd find me standing at the kitchen sink, crying silently. "How you doing, Mom?" taking my hand and squeezing it. "You okay, Mom?"

I was open and honest with Johnny and the others about my feelings and insecurities, and I think this gave them the freedom to feel okay about expressing their feelings.

I can still picture my mother in her small, modest house, knitting perfectly even rows . . . sweaters, blankets . . . amid total cleanliness and order. The orderly life didn't come easily for me.

I managed to survive the pain of my low self-image as long as I stayed at home. But whenever we were out in public—at church, at a restaurant, or at a party with friends—I tortured myself with comparisons.

I must weigh 30 pounds more than Jane. My eyes are small and beady compared to Sue's.

"The image-managers encourage the individual to fashion himself into a smooth coin, negotiable in any market."
—John Gardner

What I'd give for a beautiful tan like Sally's.

Why can't I be bright and entertaining like Mary?

I'd go home from such events hating myself, feeling guilty for being envious.

My friends never saw this side of me. I felt I had to hide it, or they wouldn't have liked me. It worked because, despite my hidden fears and insecurities, I was well-liked, and some people even told me I was wonderful.

They couldn't see the suffering—I had it too well hidden. Pretense had become a way of life.

Some people even said I was attractive. Even so, I only saw an overweight, matronly woman with pasty white skin, hairy arms, too-curly hair, still-crooked teeth, and now, weird feet.

I made my husband the ultimate authority in my life; I made sure he went shopping with me whenever I needed clothes. I gave him the deciding vote on what I wore. On his growing attorney's income, I could afford a few of the latest fashions—and I often succumbed to the trends. I didn't know how atrocious my clothes were. The silver lame' square-necked evening gown, or the burgundy culottes with the bulky knit pink pullover sweater. I had a closet full of clothes but nothing to wear. I'd wind up in a shocking pink muu-muu, because I thought it would make me look feminine and exciting to John. The navy blue and white striped pantsuit was chosen because he liked the sophisticated, traditional look. Both outfits were disastrous for my coloring. I knew I was looking worse all the time.

It wasn't until years later that I realized everything depends on point of view. Most experts who give opinions do so from their own perspective, which is contaminated by their prejudices and instincts about themselves. Intuitively John knew that silver lame' would have been gorgeous on him if he'd been the other gender. He simply didn't know yet which colors complemented me the most. We struggled together to know each other and ourselves better. The struggle was a silent one.

The only one who ever said anything was Johnny. He never failed. "Hey, that's a great new dress, Mom!" Despite this encouragement from a loyal son, I knew I didn't look good. I stayed home in my bathrobe as often as I could find an excuse to. And then, too, I was "sick" a lot. It was when we were with other people that I had to come face to face with myself—and I hated that.

One of the best examples of seeing myself happened quite innocently. I was always on diets—a continuing effort to *win*. The pounds yo-yoed up and down all the time, but when I was on the successful end of two weeks of starving I, for a brief time, felt better about my self-control and life seemed to be improving. I was doing so well I even began to see myself as a good mother.

Now, "good" mothers (one of my illusions) have warm, homemade cookies waiting for their children when they come home from school! So, I busied myself making cookies, singing and dancing happily as I was making them.

Then an hour before the children came home, the smell of those cookies got to me, and I ate three. Remember, I had been starving for two weeks!

Two minutes later the guilts attacked: "Cookies make you fat" or "You are stupid if you can't control yourself from eating a cookie while on a diet."

After an hour I lost the battle and was in a heavy self-hate mode. I was stupid, ugly, fat, uncontrolled and totally miserable again.

I thought I might as well eat a few more cookies

and grab a few minutes of pleasure. I could try being wonderful again tomorrow.

So, I was about to "sneak" more cookies when my children walked in from school. Was I angry! They caught me cookie-handed!

They knew I was dieting; why couldn't they have waited?

They asked innocently if they could go and play with friends.

"Play, is that all you ever think of? I'd give anything if just *one* of my children would come home just *one* day," my voice level raised, ". . . and ask me what they could do to help. Do you know what I've been doing all day? I've cleaned the entire house." (I had vacuumed one bedroom and the hall.)

"Do you realize what a mess *your* room is? How many times have I told you to clean your room before going to school?"

I was really saying to *myself,* "You're sloppy, lazy, thoughtless, self-centered."

But I didn't know I was talking to me, and neither did the children. They thought I was attacking them. They believed I thought they were lazy.

I should have hung a sign around my neck saying, "Mother ate three cookies, broke her diet and now hates herself." I would have hated myself less.

If I hadn't believed eating cookies was terrible, or if I had chosen not to eat cookies that day, I would have responded quite differently.

"Honey, your room is a mess. Clean it first and then you can go play."

Easy? Yes, sometimes. But the wonderful challenge is to look at the game when it isn't easy, when there is hurt inside.

I learned to do it, to meet the challenges. The first step was learning that I had the strength to do it. One night at home, when I was feeling especially lonely and awful, I pulled out my high school yearbook. There I was . . . a member of Latin Club, Girls Association President, and one of the top ten seniors scholastically in the Class of 1956. Was that really *me*?

Though I didn't look as bad in the photographs as I remembered, the camera *had* captured some of the self-doubt. I began reading what some of my old acquaintances had written about me then. I read into the night because I couldn't believe my eyes.

> "Susan, How do you stay so vivacious and look so pretty? I don't know how you do it! E. Robinson '55."

> "Susan, I think you know how much all of us wanted you in our club—but we understand the reason why you can't. If you ever get permission, let us know. Love, Donna D. '54."

> "Dear Susan, In spite of the fact that I like you so much, I guess it's only natural to envy someone who is so gifted in so many ways, and yet remains as sweet and charming as you do. B. West '56."

> "Susan, You say you need to go on a diet. I say you don't—you've got a great figure. B. Bowman '56."

"Beauty is an image of truth and therefore, if we see life steadily and see it whole, the disagreeables will evaporate as they do in a great work of art."

—John Keats

54

"Susie, I've never known anyone who has the heart you do. And I'll never forget the night of the prom. It was the first time I told you I loved you. That was the most beautiful I've ever seen you.
John '56."

"Susie, As I have stated hundreds of times, my parents adore you. You are always the shining example in our household. Since I agree with my folks, I really don't mind.
Lynda '55."

I was stunned!

That *couldn't* have been *me* they were talking about!

Why had I never really heard or believed the compliments from friends who apparently loved me after all?

Why had I so relentlessly hung on to and magnified the negative things I'd heard about myself?

Did I feel safer as a loser than as a winner?

Then what about the contradictions? How could those yearbook inscriptions be true if what my father said was true? And, come to think of it, if I was such a loser, why did my teachers praise me? Why did Lynda's parents think I was so wonderful? Why did 200 young women elect me to be Governor of Girls State? And if I was so stupid, why was I among the few women accepted to Stanford?

It was like two jigsaw puzzles mixed together. Which "pieces" fit the picture that was me and which ones didn't? It was clear that as long as I felt unacceptable inside myself, I wasn't able to acknowledge or enjoy acceptance from others.

All the heavy baggage I carried from childhood into my career as a wife and mother took its toll on my relationships with others, as evidenced by that little vignette the day the PTA President found me home in such disarray, clad in bathrobe and curlers.

It wasn't that I looked so terrible that day. The point was that I projected how awful I felt by the way I looked. My appearance reflected and reinforced my life-long lack of self-esteem, and I was taking it out on everyone around me.

How could I think about others when I was so caught up with myself?

In all my self-consciousness, I began to wonder how strong a correlation there was between the way I looked and the way I felt about myself. If I could look better, would I be less self-conscious and anxious? I discovered that a pattern had developed from my feelings of worthlessness; a vicious cycle that went round and round, year after year.

The cycle:

Low self-esteem . . . lethargy . . . disregard for personal appearance . . . withdrawal . . . anger . . . damaged relationships . . . loneliness . . . even lower self-esteem.

I decided I'd better pull myself together once and for all, if only for the sake of my family. They were growing up, and I wanted them to feel proud of me. At that point, I could justify looking good for someone else even if *I* wasn't worth the effort.

A victim of the 1950s mentality, I figured all I would need in order to look and feel like Grace Kelly or Doris Day was to lose thirty-five pounds and take beauty classes to learn how to cover up my flaws with good makeup and the latest fashions.

I tried every hair style, every new fad in makeup and clothing, every color that was "in." But I never got the right look. I gravitated to every lecture, class and book on beauty and self-image. There was always a new "expert" on the scene. It all sounded great, but none of it had a permanent effect. (Where *was* my Fairy Godmother?)

We were living in California—our son John was 9, and our fifth child, Trevor, was just a baby—when I decided I needed to take drastic measures. I read about a famous modeling school close by. It seemed ridiculous for a 27-year-old woman with five children to even consider enrolling, but I wanted to do just that.

John was upset that I would even bring it up. I had just completed another course that had not done me any visible good, and here I was determined to take yet *another*.

He was as tired of my fruitless search as I was, but I assured him (and myself) that this would bring about "real" changes at last.

I enrolled.

Imagine my relief to finally be in the hands of "authorities" who could tell me exactly how to dress and apply makeup! I had been so low, anything would be a lift to me, and it was. Best of all, I finally had the incentive to lose weight. It was no

"We can be knowledgeable with other men's knowledge but we cannot be wise with other men's wisdom."

—Michel de Montaigne

special diet. I just cut back drastically on calories.

I believed every word my "stylish" instructors said. "You must carry or wear gloves everywhere you go." . . . "Always wear pink or white lipstick." . . . "Wear jackets long enough to cover your heavy thighs." I dutifully obeyed, though my instincts told me differently on many of their blanket commands.

Of the eight women in my class, I knew less than most of them about beauty techniques. I was embarrassed and could never picture myself modeling along side any of them.

I learned the right way to sit, stand, walk gracefully, exercise, apply lots of makeup and wear all the current fashions. Six months and $1,000 later, I looked like a department store mannequin with artificial-looking makeup and beehive hairdo, complete with the popular, but tacky, short skirt.

At graduation exercises for all the classes at the school, I won the "Eliza" Award (named for Eliza Doolittle of "My Fair Lady") for accomplishing the greatest change (a put-down in itself). I arrived as a nobody but left a real Somebody—from *their* perspective.

My new plastic "Hollywood look" proved more unsettling to me than my former uniform of bathrobe, slippers and pincurls.

But my glamorous look was "in," and I made a shakey attempt at tearoom and photographic modeling, feeling resentful toward the fashion industry that had taken my husband's place in my mind as the "final authority" on myself.

My inner voice shouted, "This is not me! Who am I kidding?" I didn't listen.

I fooled my friends. They said I looked wonderful. I knew they must have been referring to my weight loss, because the rest was wrong.

Still swimming around in my head was all the professional advice that was supposed to make me beautiful. You should wear vertical stripes to make you appear taller." (I feel like a clown in stripes.) "Wear black to make you appear more slim and sophisticated." (I feel awful in black.) "Rat your hair high to appear taller." (What about the smooth pageboy I always wanted?) "Wear blue eye shadow to bring out your eyes." (Even though it makes me look like a reptile?)

All the experts' advice fought with my instinctive yearning for refinement and classic good taste.

Looking back, the only positive outcome from finishing school was that I lost all that weight. But I did that by myself. My own motivation was at work there. I simply cut back on my eating and exercised faithfully!

Though slimmer, I was now projecting a false, painted image that confused and frightened me. I was afraid of being discovered for who I really was. *Whoever* I was.

Who, I still didn't know. What was I supposed to look like? Did anybody besides me even care? *(Where was my Fairy Godmother?)*

This "new look" and inner confusion made things even worse for the family. With my self-

"I was all VOGUE on the outside and all VAGUE on the inside."

—*Anonymous*

respect at a new low, it was hard for me to respect others, even my loved ones, and I wondered how they could respect me.

Chapter Six

W E had an opportunity to move from California to Canada where my husband had been sent on a special assignment.

Leaving everything behind, we found ourselves in strange new surroundings, and I found myself even more in need of confidence. With my husband so busy with a demanding new schedule, I felt desperate to keep up with him and be the supportive wife.

To avoid being swallowed up by my growing fear and self-doubt, I plunged into a frantic schedule of traveling to distant meetings with John, cooking and hostessing for huge groups of people, carting children off to ice skating and piano lessons, caring for our toddler, and after a while another new baby on the way.

All this "busy"ness was a vain attempt to escape the haunting voices of my early life. "Who do you think you are, the Queen of Sheba?" "What a baby!" "When will you ever grow up?"

At the same time there were many positive things happening in my life: new friends, newly discovered strengths—among them, my ability to deal with large groups of people—strangers at that!

Two inner voices waged war. One said, "You're a nothing and always will be"—the other told me, "You are strong and so much is expected of you." Self-doubt—worry about whether I could measure up to what everyone needed from me—haunted my days and threatened to eat me alive if I slowed down for one minute. Nervous, afraid and vulnerable, my only solace was my family, whose near round-the-clock activities drove me from task to task.

The weight I'd lost I regained with two pregnancies. I let my hair grow long, thinking I'd look younger. I wore bright, dramatic colors and prints that were strong in order to compensate for my insecurities.

To some of my acquaintances, I might have appeared to have it all together. I worked hard at the pretense while I was dying inside. It was a good thing I had so much opportunity to take care of others—because I couldn't face myself.

By this time we had seven children ranging in age from newborn to fifteen years. Our youngest was born after five months of frightening health problems. We wondered if the baby would survive, and if she did, if she would have severe handicaps. Her normal birth was a relief and a joy to the family. The five months of living in fear gave me new insights. I appreciated each of my children so much more, and I marveled at the miracle of a healthy child.

One day, when this daughter was nearly two years old, we were driving into town together. I remembered what a rough pregnancy I had had with her and how frightened I had felt about possibly losing her. What a miracle it seemed that she was there with me. Emotion welled up inside of me, and I turned to her and said, "I love you, Amanda!"

She looked up at me and with assuredness replied, "Everybody loves Amanda!"

I was stunned! I couldn't believe my ears. It seemed so natural for her to be so sure. I knew there was something profound about what she had said, but I didn't fully understand what it was at that moment.

I remember lying awake at night over the next few weeks with her words ringing in my mind, "Everybody loves Amanda." Why was she so sure? Why was I so surprised? Why didn't I feel loved as she did? Why was I so unsure?

Slowly I gained the insight that turned my whole life around: *NO ONE IS BORN WITH A POOR SELF-IMAGE.*

I had accepted the negatives as my cross to bear; I had chosen to accept them and then covered them with a smile.

Well, then, if I wasn't born with a poor self-image, if I had learned negatives, I could also unlearn them. First I had to find their source. But, did I really want to find who I was? The unknown can be frightening.

Amanda seemed so happy with herself, a perfect example. I began to listen to other little children.

If you go up to a small child, say a three-year-old boy, and you ruffle his curly hair as you walk by him and say, "You're terrific," what does he do? He simply shrugs his shoulders and says, "I know," and goes on about his play.

If there hasn't been infant or child abuse in a home, little children know they're terrific, wonderful and beautiful. They know they can do anything.

"The more faithfully you listen to the voice within you, the better you will hear what is sounding outside."
—Dag Hammerskjold

If you say to a little girl, "You're so pretty," she looks up at you and grins from ear to ear as if to say, "Isn't it wonderful, you're so perceptive!" And you grin back happily, knowing she knows pure truth.

Amanda's comment to me showed special confidence. There is no conceit in such a child's self-image; there is only security, only reality, only instinctive understanding that she is wonderful and special.

And I don't think that confidence is ill-placed. Wordsworth wrote that we are born ". . . trailing clouds of glory." What little child is not beautiful and special? What baby girl is not a wonderful miracle of life—a marvelous creature endowed with intellect and spirit and warmth and humor? Such gifts are our birthright. No matter what else we might come to perceive about ourselves, our essential, inherent beauty and value survive with us.

The only thing holding us down, then, is our ability to see what is really there. Inhibitions pile up, don't they? And doubts and defenses are sure to follow life's disappointments. Over the years some of us can collect a rather overwhelming pile of negatives. When these negatives become the strongest influence in our life, what is it that will bring to life faded dreams and dimmed realities?

Choice! We can choose to change our perceptual filter so that instead of hearing and seeing only the negatives, we can choose to see and hear ourselves, as Amanda did.

"*Everybody* loves Amanda!"

Her words had charged me with electricity. But

if you had asked me why, I couldn't have told you. The truthfulness of what she said was absolute.

"Everybody loves Amanda!" How could a tiny little girl come up with such a pearl? The answer is, she had no concept of anything but love about herself.

Her high regard for herself was inborn!

If *no one is born with a poor self-image* that means not even Susie! Not even you!

My awareness grew. If I had not been born with a poor self-image and low self-esteem, then I had created a false Susan. The fat, ugly Susan was an illusion I had *chosen* to believe. I chose that version to protect myself from people who might reject me if I loved them—or me—too much, too openly. By hiding inside my ugly self-image, I didn't have to share myself with others around me—even the people I loved.

My next step was to understand that since I had chosen to believe an illusion, I could choose to not believe it anymore. *My Fairy Godmother was not coming!*

I could choose a new reality. But what was reality? My journey was just beginning. I was ready to look within me and to listen to a "felt" sense of who I actually was behind those inner-conflicting voices.

The Fairy Godmother is *not* coming!"

Chapter Seven

T HE days following my discovery were spent getting settled in a new home: we had returned to the USA. John was busy with a new career, and the children bustled about with school activities and new friends.

A touch of calm soothed my life, the result of knowing I had the power to change after all. I could be everything I had dreamed of being.

I enrolled in a college course in human behavior and learned to eliminate irrelevant thought patterns. I became aware of the process of change—*who I* could change and how.

But this was to be an emotion-charged year in my life. No sooner had I felt my burden lifting than our oldest son, Johnny, was killed in an automobile accident. It occurred late one night as he was on his way home from performing in a musical play. He was seventeen, a college freshman. My best buddy through all my years of pain was gone, just when I finally had some good things to share with him. He had always seen that beautiful part of me that I had just now caught a glimpse of.

The weeks and months that followed were a study in contrasts—agonies and ecstasies, pain and numbness, sadness and joy, darkness and light. I remember the horror of the house seeming so empty, and yet the rooms also rang out with memories of the bustle and all the noise of living together. How dark and lonely our bedroom was at night, and yet, as I closed my eyes, everything seemed bright and alive as the past played over and over on a screen in my mind.

There were many days when I just laid on the bed and sobbed. There was so much emotion to let out. Our family was abruptly and, for this life, permanently separated. But in many ways we were never more bound, more unified.

The children suffered without Johnny. Amanda and Katie prayed for him every night. Trevor's usual good behavior changed for the worse at school. And Erica, then in high school, asked, "Mom, will we ever be happy again?" I thought to myself, "I'm not sure."

"People are like stained-glass windows; They sparkle and shine when the sun is out, But when the darkness sets in, their true Beauty is revealed only if there is a light From within."
—Elisabeth Kubler-Ross

It doesn't take a death in the family for a person to experience these contrasts. Most of us have good days and bad days, happy moments and frustrating times. What we need to do is fully feel, then examine all the good and bad, happy and sad, frightening and calm feelings and learn to choose to be more aware of the positive. We can only do this as we learn to release the negatives. What must happen before positive beliefs can become knowledge and actions? What if we never have really let ourselves care about anyone, ever? How do we love if we've never seen or tasted love? How do we learn to love ourselves?

How do we "feel" love? Is it like being blind and learning to know color?

One way to begin is to hurt, and/or allow ourselves to "feel" the hurt. I think I did that after John died. I hurt so much, I stopped pretending I

didn't hurt. I didn't feel like hiding anymore. I
wept outwardly, felt torn apart inwardly. It was the
beginning of getting to know "me." Inside, deep
inside, I felt I touched a bit of my own essence. I
began to want to know more. I wanted to "live." I
wanted to "feel" all kinds of feelings, not just the
hurt.

HEALING

The angriness poured out
    And beat itself to death,
        Pounding and hurting.
Then the wound lay open and tired.
    How long this battle had been fought!
        How deep the struggle.
The cries of war were finally silenced
    But the weariness kept weeping,
        Cleansing the wound.
Please let me rest now . . .
    Just for awhile . . .
        Let me heal.

Trusting not my own understandings,
    I cried out
        And He heard me.
I knew He knew my heart;
    I felt Him near.
        I crept into His cradle.
And felt the calm of the storm's end
    And for awhile
        I was healing.
The warmth moved through me,
    And my heart and mind became one
        In that moment.

The surge of life's energy
    Echoed from a memory,
        Giving love.
I am love; it's there.
    My body is alive,
        Feeling the now.
With each touch, each glance
    I breathed . . .
        I lived.
Touch me tenderly
    As I heal and
        Let me not wound Thee.

—S.W., April '85

Albert Schweitzer expresses what was ignited within me:

> Affirmation of life is the spiritual act by which man ceases to live unreflectively and begins to devote himself to his life with reverence in order to raise it to its true value. To affirm life is to deepen, to make more inward, and to exalt the will to live.

Profound words. Don't try to understand them; merely sense his urgent plea for us to affirm the feelings of aliveness within.

The tragedy left me newly dedicated to change my life. After several months of feeling my way through the darkness, I finally felt ready to begin.

I plunged back into my work as a mother with new enthusiasm. I felt a new kind of love arise. I shed the extra pounds. I took the best of what I had learned from all the "beauty experts" I had gone to and somehow had the courage to apply only what *instinctively* felt best to me in makeup and clothing.

I had my hair re-styled by a relative, a cosmetologist, who encouraged me to do something different. Just for fun, she cut my hair to a new length, stopping at the jawline. It looked great! For some reason it worked!

My new positive self-image was finally showing in my physical appearance, and people began to take notice. "Susie, is that *you*?" I would hear at the grocery store. At a PTA meeting: "Susan, you've come to life; what's happened?"

To my amazement, I was asked to coordinate a class in personal development to hundreds of women as part of an on-going training program for my church.

The idea was for me to give the women good, basic knowledge on how to improve their appearance with the accent on classic beauty traditions. I liked that approach, for I had been betrayed so many times by "current trends" that had made me look worse instead of better.

I poured myself into the task of assisting in the design of the self-improvement curriculum for women.

As the director, I had a lot to give, but I still felt inadequate and ill-equipped. All my life I had blindly followed the experts and now women were looking to *me* as the expert! So much of what I had learned from beauty professionals was based on merchandising, not science. I forced myself to refine the best of the knowledge I had collected over the years.

Other instructors came into the program: women experienced in nutrition, poise, make-up, hairstyling, fashion and wardrobe planning.

Together we worked on defining techniques to help the women in our classes find the best ways to present themselves.

In the process of giving, everything continued to come together for me personally. My shorter hair enhanced my features, and I was keeping my weight down for the first time in my life.

One of our instructors had taken college courses on the science of color, and I was told about her fascinating information concerning prismatic color law. I asked if she would share these principles with our board.

This was exciting for me. I had always known that the colors I wore had a profound effect not only on the way I looked, but the way I felt. But thanks to some misguidance from some "experts," I had never really learned which colors were best for me.

The scientific approach to color was of particular interest to me because on separate occasions I had been professionally analyzed by the "seasonal" color consultants. The first time I was labeled a "Spring" and told I should wear bright greens and yellows. Then another expert told me I was a "Summer" and should wear soft blues, pinks and pale greys.

Not only were the two consultants' advice in conflict with each other, but both were in conflict with my instinctive feelings. I wasn't comfortable in *any* of the light, bright Spring-Summer colors.

Later, a third "expert" from another variation in a stream of color systems told me I was an "Autumn." Now I felt closer to home. I felt the rich, warm shades suited me well, no doubt about it.

But in the wide array of autumn colors, which were best? Dark brown? Olive green? Camel? Rust? A few months later I was told I was a Summer again—back to the light blues! Was I ever confused!

My pending experience with the scientific approach to color soon cleared that up, however.

Using fabric swatches in several dozen colors, a board of women sat in front of mirrors under good light and, one by one, discovered how each color blended or clashed with her own natural coloring.

This was different from any other "color" coding experiences in that I understood there was a science to color. Somehow that knowledge alone took the expertise away from any one person or "expert." I could certainly see the physical difference colors made, but my inner feelings were getting in the way. Everyone in the room unanimously agreed about what was right for me. But the colors they all liked on me were ugly to me. I fought back the tears and just nodded my agreement. Why was I feeling so emotional? It was *only* color.

In the weeks that followed, I looked at those "ugly" colors and began to hear the voices in my past, all that "others" had said about those colors. Once again, I was aware of how I had chosen to believe what others had said, even though my inner self said, "No!" Was it only an illusion that some colors were ugly and some were beautiful?

The truth is that all colors are wonderful. I finally could acknowledge that fact and felt a sense of relief. I began asking myself, "How do *I* feel about color and why do I feel that way?" I walked through stores, looked at nature, looked at other people and simply let myself feel—for *real* this time.

I started picking up objects just to touch the color. There *was* a magnetic link to something in me.

My feelings, in time, made my decision. My instincts were the confirming factor in how I felt connected to color. I felt in harmony with my color selections and not just in outward appearance. Oh, it was possible to see how my hair and eyes and the basic pigmentation of my skin could dictate the colors I should wear in make-up and clothing—and this would all be based on science, not season—but that was not what created the changes in me. The real change came about when I heard a voice I hadn't attended to before.

As I slowly allowed myself to savor feelings—the whole rainbow, acknowledged and loved, good and bad—curiously my awareness and ability to sense grew dramatically. Color is powerful, and I was being affected.

One day when I was shopping, I happened to pass by Ladies Sportswear at the top of the escalator. Out of the corner of my eye I caught a glimpse of a blouse. I was about to pass by it, but suddenly my feet turned me around, and my body had no choice but to go along with them. I picked the blouse up and took it with me to a mirror where I could hold it up to me. I felt a gasp rise like a bubble from inside—I was so excited. I saw my eyes dancing; I

felt beautiful with that blouse. I chastised myself,
"You came here to buy a wedding present. Don't
get distracted." Back went the blouse, and I forced
my attention to Housewares.

While making my purchase—a bud vase—and
having it gift wrapped, I rationalized why it would be
all right for me to look at that blouse again, check
the price—it might be on sale. Also, we were
planning a trip to California in a week, and I needed
a blouse. Most compelling—I hadn't had the desire
to purchase anything since Johnny had died. I
needed the blouse to cheer me up.

When I saw the blouse, I had no more need for
reasons; the blouse was me, chosen by me because of
the way it made me feel: calm, sure, beautiful. The
choice had nothing to do with my husband, friend or
any expert. I knew it was right for me. The test:
when I tried it on I didn't see the blouse, I saw me.

But everything changed when I got
outside—wearing the blouse. I looked down at it and
realized it was an ugly, non-descript color—like Dijon
mustard. John would hate it. But my expert friend
would tell me it was right. Facts and reason again
and conflicting opinions, too. For a moment I felt
the confusion of how to please all those voices. But
the attention I had given my feelings paid off. I felt
myself actually stroking the sleeves of that blouse and
a voice inside spoke peacefully to me.

Instead of chastisement I was hearing a friend.
The voice inside liked what I was on the outside. I
was no longer at war with me. I did it! I learned to
listen to me.

*"A woman has first
to discover her
personality and dress
in harmony with
that."*
　　　—Balenciaga

Chapter Eight

Months passed and I grew in my ability to process feelings evoked by color. Wonderful friends kept coming into my life. They loved me even when I was running away and hiding. They acknowledged my bravery when I tried new things; and they challenged me to look inside myself even more courageously. They laughed *with* me as I learned self-discovery isn't terrible after all.

They made it easy for me to see my real "put-down" enemy as a part of me. It was a wonderful part, willing to poke its head up so I could see what I was swinging at. Discovering the negatives, learning to control them, is how we grow. The critical me was a part that wanted to be seen so I could meet the challenge of overcoming problems and win.

The new knowledge about prismatic color law was much more than a simple matter of wearing any one grouping of colors—not all of them looked that great on me. It turned out that there were some colors which actually made a difference; colors I'd been told by some "experts" I should *never* wear. But I felt terrific in them: muted shades of khaki green, putty, warm grey, pale rust . . . shades and intensities that blended with my natural coloring.

This color process has been known for centuries by those who have studied pigment color theory. It is more complex and thorough than other color systems because it is based on the physical laws which create color as light filters through a prism. The cause and effect of color can be seen and rationally understood.

My memory flashed back to a khaki green dress I had sewn years before. The color wasn't at all fashionable at the time. But I wore that dress until it was threadbare. Why was I so attached to it? I must have instinctively known it was right—I felt comfortable and "at home" with the color.

Color science *really* did make sense, after all. And technical as it seemed, even *I* could understand it!

After learning the basic principles I felt like a little child re-discovering my best colors. The trouble was, eighty percent of the clothing in my closet felt wrong. And not just because of color.

The lines and styles I'd been wearing were all wrong for my figure.

I later learned (through reading about anatomy studies by Michelangelo) that by using the principle of body proportion in conjunction with head length, some style-lines would distract from imbalances in my figure. Well-chosen clothing could accentuate my positive features or give the illusion of balance to an unbalanced figure. I stopped hating my body and began dealing with my "problem" bust and hips, and my long waist and short legs. It was a new perspective that didn't say short legs were ugly, they were just short! The challenge was how to help them appear longer or how to shorten other areas to balance them. That was easier than learning how to stop hating them. Those short legs are part of the total me that I can now balance and love.

If someone says they have long arms, I always want to ask them if someone told them that. Or is it an instinctive awareness? Knowing if our arms are long or short comes from knowing our entire body proportion.

Start with your head length and see how many "head-lengths" tall you are. The average American woman is 7.5 heads tall and most models are over eight heads tall.

If you have a short head, you may appear taller than you actually measure. If you have a long head, you may appear shorter than you measure.

Now look at your arms and consider their appearance in relation to your body. In the science of art, arms can be proportionately created by understanding the science of anatomy, knowing how many head lengths an arm must be to balance the body.

Of course, we can't change our arm length the way artists do on paper, but we can be aware of lines in clothing and jewelry and wear things which create the appearance of longer or shorter arms.

You already have instinctive, unconscious clues as to how to create this balance. If you always like to roll up or push up long sleeves, you probably have long arms. If you don't feel comfortable in sleeveless clothes, even on very hot days, it may be because you have long arms. If you like wide contrasting cuffs on long sleeves, you may have long arms, too.

This is just a taste of the understanding that can come from study and awareness of what you already know instinctively. Our instincts are working all the time to bring us into balance with ourselves. We

"Charge all things you fashion with a breath of your own spirit!"
            —Gibran

waste energy on trying to balance our bodies with other people's ideas of what we should do.

Shopping and clothes have taken on a whole new perspective for me. Jealousy and envy of other women disappeared as I learned to appreciate my coloring and my body. I could also enjoy other people and their uniqueness. Best of all, I learned how beautifully intuitive I had been with myself at times.

"Whoever hath a good presence and a good fashion carries continual letters of recommendation."
—Bacon

It was wonderful! My well-worn khaki green dress with a pleated bodice and soft, flowing skirt were all perfect lines for my coloring and my figure.

I also found the same universal laws of line, proportion and balance apply to hairstyle and makeup. Once I digested the principles, I let my instincts take over. Armed with new knowledge, and with the help of hairdressers who would listen to what I wanted, my hair slowly took shape to create a balance with my facial features.

I also experimented with makeup in my new-found colors—again letting my instincts take over, using principles of art. I added contour to my pasty white cheeks, drama to my ordinary eyes, found a way to detract from the potato nose, and chose lipstick color values that wouldn't call attention to *semi-straight* teeth.

Much to John's mixed emotions, my wardrobe began to change dramatically. Out went the red and white polka dot dress, the kelly green and black knit, the grey pantsuit!

I put myself together, piece by piece. It took about a year, because this time I had determined I'd do it *right* and that I would listen to my inner voice.

Chapter Nine

Discovering my best image was like winning a marathon. And I wasn't the only one who was thrilled.

Friends didn't recognize me. "Susie, is that *you?* You look fantastic—what have you *done?*"

No one could pinpoint specific changes I'd made because all the changes were so in harmony with my personality, coloring, features and figure—nothing stood out. Everything blended into the total new look. And the look was finally *right.*

My parents response to my transition was "Susan, you look too thin. You must not be eating enough. You don't take care of yourself, always overmatching." There was a day when I would have felt they were insensitive because they couldn't see and appreciate the changes in me. But today I recognize their special way of showing concern and love for me.

My sister, Monica, was wonderful, very kind and complimentary, as usual.

I must admit that my husband was turned off at first by my new colors. (They aren't the colors he connects with, that's why!) But he grew to admire my new look. He's sometimes non-verbal about his feelings, but I could read a lot in his approving smile.

The changes at first were small but each step was so important. The physical changes on the outside always surfaced parallel to the changes on the inside.

John enjoyed my new confidence in the beginning, but soon realized this was not the same girl he married. I could only agree, quite happily.

For John, happiness with the changes in me was fleeting and erratic at best. He sometimes rejoiced with me as I surmounted many new challenges. But our life of routine was gone. I was no longer submerged in the endless inner game with myself so my reactions became totally unpredictable.

I confused this lovely man with a lot of changing. I disrupted his expectations of life with me.

But, I was finally learning to love myself.

For me, the most important change was the intangible change—the new radiance that filled the once empty caverns inside me. Finally I could concentrate my thoughts and feelings on others and forget about myself!

The magic in finding what I really looked like was that, at last, all the good there was in me was being accurately portrayed in my appearance. The beauty was in the *balance* between long-dormant feelings of self-worth and a matching outward appearance. This balance created a congruency which I called *Image Integrity*. (This concept became the focus for the curriculum I had been working on.)

I was amazed that I didn't have to look anything like Farrah Fawcett, Bo Derek, Doris Day or my idol, Princess Grace. I could look like *myself* and be beautiful (*without* the Fairy Godmother!).

When I decided not to choose to believe the

negative voices any longer, I actually heard the positives. My appearance was beginning to validate the reality within. I suspect the positives were always there and even voiced by my father and the many other significant people in my life, but my ears had only one channel tuned in, somewhere between zero and minus ten.

Deep down I always believed that my father was a warm and caring person . . . he just didn't want anyone to know it! His energies were drained just dealing with his own pain. I reflect often now on a statement made in the film *On Golden Pond* in reference to the cantankerous old man: "He's not yelling at you, he's yelling at life. He's still trying to find his way."

As I matured, I realized through counseling and special training a very important fact. *I* was the one who believed my father's messages were negative. If I looked back on many of my childhood experiences, I could now begin to see the positives that had been there. A conversation with a counselor about my crooked teeth and my father's attitude toward braces was very revealing.

"Why didn't your father want you to have perfectly straight teeth?" she asked.

"Because he was a dictator. He always told me how I *should* feel, what I *should* think, and what I *should* be," was my angry reply. "Anything else was stupid."

"Suppose your perspective was just an illusion," she said. "What other reason could there be for acting the way he did?"

"I don't know. He was so mean. I wanted braces for years and then when he gave in, he had to have the last word and do it *his* way," I said impatiently.

"It seemed very important to him—worth the risk of making you angry with him," she replied reflectively. "What could he have wanted that would be important enough to take that risk?"

I suddenly felt a rush of tears. "He loved me!" I exclaimed. "He did love me, so much he wanted me to be unique and not look like everyone else."

My mind opened to the truth. "He actually saw my individuality and only wanted my physical self to reflect this uniqueness," I sighed longingly.

She agreed, "That's a lot of real love."

This discovery didn't change the events of my childhood or how I saw them. The real monster had been my self-perpetuating fears and loneliness. I had believed I was *not* loveable, so I could *not* see the love that was there.

I wanted to change my father (and others) so they would show me they loved me. Of course, it needed to be in a way I could see it.

It never happened.

I have slowly acknowledged that we can't change others; we can only change ourselves. This awareness was startling and intriguing.

What baffled me was that the changes in me and my new look had been largely inspired by my own instincts. I had sensed all along what was right for me, but had been side-tracked by an irrational compulsion to follow the "experts," most of whom turned out to be wrong about me.

Clearly, I couldn't change just because someone cut my hair or showed me which colors were right. Change occurred because I combined some basic knowledge about the universal laws of art with my instincts and had the courage to "go for it."

And if I can do it, *anyone* can do it. You can.

The technical knowledge required for this make-over (prismatic color law and line and proportion principles) is so important that I have devoted my life to teaching it. You need only remember, beyond this technical knowledge, the sense of self is simply the courage to listen—very carefully—and to not be afraid to hear and see your own beauty.

My 30-year make-over taught me many lessons.

It needn't have taken so long.

If I can be beautiful, despite a long list of physical flaws, so can you.

If I, who had no self-confidence, can respond to an instinctive belief in myself and become the ultimate authority on myself as beautiful, so can you. Success comes in "cans"—not in "can'ts."

I can't conduct a make-over for another woman, just as no one could have done it for me. But after my own change took place, countless women asked me for guidance—so I began giving public lectures, then seminars.

When I'm instructing, I don't tell any woman what her flaws are or what to change. I teach basic information so that *she* can find her own best image and make her own statement. For only when *she* takes charge will it mean anything to her.

Always remember self-improvement is a joyous journey, not a destination.

Though I have changed remarkably, I haven't arrived. I hope there is no arrival. I am enjoying every day of the journey.

As with any journey, half the fun is the getting there, especially if *you* are in charge of the itinerary. It's also more fun when friends journey together.

The more you're involved, the more fun it is. The beauty experts have a lot of fun and sometimes we think it's at our expense. We don't appreciate their real function, which is to provide us with a wonderful palette from which we can choose what feels best for each of us. Sometimes it's easy to lose sight of the gifts the fashion experts have for us. We believe we must make them our directors and fear that we will become zeroes if we don't follow their dictates. The fact of the matter is that some "experts," as well as family members and friends, get their kicks out of telling us what to do. It's a real ego trip, that's for sure, but it can only happen if we invite it. Ultimately each of us decides whether or not we will allow our inner-self awareness the freedom to live or repress it in favor of an outside authority figure.

I'm certain there are some of those experts, professional and non-professional, who would like to take the credit for the changes I made. The truth is that everyone in my life has made a contribution to what I am today. And I am grateful to those people who cared so much about me to take an interest and to give of themselves.

But the ultimate change came about because of a resolute courage within *me*.

This is the timeless beauty secret I have to share with every woman: *You* can become the authority on *yourself*, and when you do—when you are finally free—*you* will deserve all the credit.

It is not easy. It wasn't for me; it may not be for you, but it certainly is worth it!

All my life, before the metamorphosis, I had been tied to what others said. Everyone else was smarter; I was a nobody. No one forced me into that role; I chose it freely. You have the same choice; who will *you* be?

My story is certainly no fairy tale, but it's no tragedy either. Part of me caused me to think, feel, look and act in an unbecoming way, to project an inaccurate image of my true self.

I know better now. I am discovering the answers to questions that used to plague me: Who am I really? What is this game I'm playing?

Now I know the unknown was more frightening than the reality.

I know now I cannot change my parents. I cannot change my husband. I cannot change my children. I cannot change my friends. My miracle is that I no longer want to change any of them. I know I want only to love them. I want to support, encourage and lift them. I want to make a difference in their lives, a positive difference.

I can only change me. Knowing this, I can put my energies where I can succeed. I experienced failure when I tried to change others or hoped for change in them. I no longer fail. Instead, I experience little successes with my own growth daily, because I constantly have new challenges.

My tenacity, loyalty, caring, emotionality, industry, energy—all the ingredients that make up my unique being—once were perceived as being flaws. *I* perceived them that way. I saw them as making me ugly.

Once I tenaciously blamed other people for the way I felt. I saw my own ugly traits in them. But my inner self recognized them in me, too—and a deadly game began. There was no fun in playing the game. It wasn't just a challenge to improve—it was a war that couldn't be won. The enemy was me.

I didn't recognize the enemy. I thought it was all those who were undiscerning enough to love me.

It was hard, at first, to accept myself as the real enemy, to stop blaming others for my unhappiness. Then, when I did accept my inner self as my worst critic, my most devastating "authority," I realized what I had done to me all those years, and I couldn't forgive myself. Such betrayal! But playing against yourself that way is lonely—a self-defeating inner game.

You can only win by making the inner voice your friend. Then the conflict within can become a game, a challenge to grow. It's a game of win/win.

"Never seem more learned than the people you are with. Wear your learning like a pocket-watch and keep it hidden. Do not pull it out to count the hours, but give the time when you are asked."
—*Lord Chesterfield in letters to his son*

98

I not only forgave myself, I learned to delight in being me.   It became a game of love/love.

Memories of what I've done:
 The faces, the food, the countryside, the cities.
I'm bringing home
 To those I love all this . . .
Which spoke truth to my soul
 And sang to my heart.

Memories of what I've been:
 Learning, caring, loving and giving . . .
I'm coming home
 To go on discovering . . .
I've only begun to see
 The real possibilities.

What was familiar before
 Now seems foreign . . .
What will the blending be
 Of the old and the new?
Life's refining process
 Includes everything I do.

 —S.W., Oct. '84

If you wish to share your journey with Susan, or to obtain more information about instructional courses or materials, you can write to her at:

Crown Regency, Ltd.
Suite 305
400 Madison Avenue
New York, New York 10017